P9-BIR-190

Praise for
Light the Way

All through *Light the Way* we encounter our humanness reflected in brilliant color. Barbara Toboni's newest collection of poems turns daily life into magical wonder, full of sights, sound and the tactile rush of the wave as it recedes across the sand. Toboni's nature-observant eye and whimsical mind have conspired to make us laugh, to make us cry, and to offer us a joy-filled homage to politics, love, aging, buying a dress, pets, cars, even sweeping the floor—all illuminated through her "Pink Rose" glasses. Aptly named, *Light the Way* presents a world that's softer, more hopeful than headlines suggest. Reading this collection will convince us "to surrender our burdens" and see the sublime in the ordinary, the blessedness of life.

— Ana Manwaring
Author, editor, teacher

Barbara Toboni's *Light the Way* is a rainbow of different kinds of poems and subject matters. In fact, many of the poems are laced with colors brightening the vivid imagery, as in "Oh Orange." "When the orange/explosion happened/in the 60s/I lived in Orange, California." There are many other delightful poems in which the colors "light the way," in addition to strong imagery and narrative elements.

Barbara Toboni's poems are not limited to colors and imagery. Many poems play on the sounds of language, such as the slightly whimsical "The Party," with its rich use of consonance assonance, and alliteration.

Given all this virtuosity, the poems in *Light the Way* are lovely in their colors, imagery, and sounds, and also treat, clearly and elegantly, a range of universal topics. This book will delight and move the hearts of its readers many time over.

—Gary Silva
Poet Laureate, Napa County, 2008-10

Barbara Toboni's poems in *Light the Way* tap gently from a place that resembles the here and now but is a more magical locale. Her elegant stanzas offer subtle flavors to sip and savor as she presents ordinary moments in ways that arrest, sometimes with a whisper and sometimes with a *ka-pow*!

—Laura McHale Holland,
Author of *Reversible Skirt* and *Resilient Ruin*.

Light the Way

Barbara Toboni

A Collection of Poetry

BT PRESS | NAPA, CA

Copyright © 2017 by Barbara Toboni

All rights reserved. No part of this publication may be reproduced, distributed or transmitted in any form or by any means, without prior written permission.

BT Press
1055 Darms Lane
Napa, CA 94558
www.barbaratoboni.com

Publishers Note: some poems have appeared in *First Press, And the Beats Go On*, and *Stolen Light*.

Book Layout © 2015 BookDesignTemplates.com
Cover photography by Barbara Toboni
Cover design by Amber Lea Starfire

Light the Way/ Barbara Toboni — 1st ed.
ISBN 978-0-9993736-0-6

To David and my two marvelous sons, Chase and Jim.

The day came when the risk to become tight in a bud was more painful than the risk it took to blossom.

—Anais Nin

Contents

On Vine Trail

The bench surrounded
by wildflowers
A slender finger of grass
pokes through wood slats
Four tiny petals flutter
Are you blue-eyed Susan
or Mary?

I daydream we
are friends
whispering secrets
I've always longed
for daughters
although I have
two marvelous sons

Tell me
your secret
I am not
blue-eyed Susan
or Mary
I am common
Mustard ♣

Woman Holding Asparagus

I'm wearing a floral print dress
Pearls around my neck
The white ivory bracelet a gift
from my husband
He bought it in an antique shop

I am standing in my sister-in-law's kitchen
holding a spear of asparagus
smiling for the camera
Perhaps the photographer asks, *What's for dinner?*
I brought asparagus, I say
I wish I knew more details about the day

All I know is the young woman is me
and she appears to be happy ❧

Daisies Lie

I grew up believing in daisies
He loves me he loves me not
That was the beginning, the hook
I want to believe in daisies
but daisies lie

Where were they when my parents divorced
Where were they when I divorced
Nowhere to be found

I start to suspect daisies lie
Loyalty, he loves me
Jealousy, loves me not
Obsession, he loves me
Infatuation, loves me not

DAISIES LIE

Gazing into blue
resolute sky each spring
passion shines
awaits my decision
I pluck a dandelion
inhale hope
exhale desire

If daisies lie
can I count on the wishes of dandelions ♣

The Party

People mingling
floating fizzling
bubbling bursting
steadily settling
finally flattening
like soda pop

Turn a Corner

I turn a corner
His kitchen full of
laughing friends
Dark-lashed
merry blue eyes
welcome me
the unexpected guest

I'm here
to see Laura...
your roommate
Awkwardness
explained
His smile
disarming

Laura appears
ready to go
You can stay
he says
Laura shrugs

I'm not here
to see him
or am I ♣

From My C Street Window

I see his sure-footed stroll
swing of arms and legs in sync
A trim-bearded man
in a hurry
to see me

I hear his energetic step
on the porch stair
solid rap at my door
A man's whistle
to fetch me

My heart skips, fingers tingle
as I twist open the door
to a good man's
bright smile
for me ❧

Hugging You

is like diving
into an envelope

Stationery
folded neatly in thirds
words tucked in

Wrapped in ribbon
for safe-keeping ⚘

Color to Wonder

I

Colors are colors
nothing else
Flavors are flavors
something else
Combine both
there's even more
As if in pink
bubblegum
could be found
Or in brown
a bar of chocolate
The trouble with green
when limes are inside
is the same as for yellow
where lemons reside
My lips start to pucker
Only orange can restore
my sanity

II

There's a notion
colors feel
Glow in fairy tales
Wicked black queen
lips purpling with passion
moans to her mirror
of lost beauty

Becomes envious
green witch
offering Snow White
luscious red apple
poison
Prince Charming
dispels curse
with gentle kiss
in time to save
happily-ever-after

Hopeful
At least that's how
yellow sees things ♣

Oh, Orange

When the orange
explosion happened
in the 60's
I lived in Orange, California

Out back
our apartment building
an orange grove
Row upon row
of forbidden fruit
Intoxicating perfume

Inside, our couch cushions
the color of grimy pennies
clashed with shag carpeting
a shade of squashed Cheetos

In the kitchen
Mom spooned instant coffee
from an orange Sanka jar
I squirted Cheese Whiz
onto Ritz Crackers
Sister slathered
fake tanning cream
tinting her skin copper

It seemed the astronauts
dumped Tang
all over our terracotta town
while rocketing to the moon ⚘

To You Yellow Broom

To you yellow broom all colorful specks
from floor, porch, and hallway
lawn chairs and driveway

To you yellow broom all silken cobwebs
including a spider
doily designer

To you yellow broom all swirling dust mites
graceful and airy
gathering fairies

To you yellow broom all sand from the beach
a glittering trail
from shovel and pail

To you yellow broom all snacking tidbits
nibbling fumbles
from cookie crumbles

To you yellow broom all kitty cat's kibble
knocked to the ground
left lying around

To you yellow broom all garden rubble
trimmings and snippings
along with vine clippings

To you yellow broom all bristles aglow
Clearing my path wherever we go ✢

Lori Sniffing Soap in the Garden Shop

She wears yellow
Says her outfit is from Easter
Wants to know if it's too conservative
Do I look like my mother?
Her mother reminds us both of Doris Day
No, that's not you I tell her

Lori's green eyes sparkle
Pearl earrings, luminescent
Her politics are not conservative
She tells me *You should vote for Bernie Sanders*
since I don't like Trump
We grumble about Hillary
Can we trust her not to lie
She says *It's a shame because we'd both love
to vote for a woman*

We want the same things
Secure borders
Terror from ISIS to end
I say *Trump seems too insensitive*
We both agree no matter who gets voted
in will be a puppet

After lunch we go to the garden shop
comment on birdfeeders, wind chimes
furniture made from wine barrels
At a display of scented soap

Lori spends too much time sniffing
I am anxious
We have to be somewhere soon
Okay, she says, *we'll go now Nervous Nelly*

We're on our way to the bookstore two blocks away
Open mic starts soon
I'm edgy about reading my poems
You should have had a glass of wine with lunch she says
I agree but wine triggers my migraines

A light brightens as I step back
I don't want to rush her
This joyful moment
Lori wearing yellow
sniffing soap at the garden shop ⚘

Red Jacket

That red jacket
atop the thrift pile
never fit right
Always thought
I'd give Red to a friend
or consign to a shop
Still waiting
Now I know why

Red reminds me of Blue
my corduroy blazer
from years ago
A five buck bargain
I wore with jeans
on cool fall evenings
out with friends

I felt secure
knowing someone had helped
rub life into Blue's sleeves
I worry about the woman
who buys Red
I want her
to be the girl I was
Shame there's not enough
wear in these stiff sleeves

Will she give Red a try
Be empowered
a chic beauty

Will I try again ✢

My Gold-toned Darling

For the past eleven years
you have never
steered me wrong

A survivor of the graceless
teen-aged driver
mom jumping speed bumps
pop hopping curbs
and the mysterious trashcan
tragedy

Do you remember your infirmity
Sputter and cough
rotten rubber tubing
no longer in production
mechanic's suggestion
glue

You are no complainer
not even when we broke
your door handle
Replaced it
with a RED one

The whole family
teased you about your age
shopped for a younger model
Found a Ford beauty

sleek lines
I couldn't resist
Trading you in wasn't easy
especially when you
raised your red handle
to bid us farewell

SORRY ♣

Pink Rose

I never liked the color pink until
this rose, stunning tint
bloomed in yellow rose's spot
Stranger to my garden

Surprise
this hue of many things
light of dawn and sun setting
apple blush
flamingo wing
Sport found in my garden

Now happy pinks pop
out at me—bubble gum
cotton candy
strawberry cream, sweet bliss
this reminder in my garden

Glow of peach, raspberry jam
pink sand beach
Christmas ham
newborn skin, goosebumps too
everywhere a hue of you
showing in my garden

Amazed and more than this
I confess my new nightdress
is pink
slippers too
Pink rose

Vineyard Leaves

Vineyard leaves are red and gold
Grapes are picked and harvest sold
The dog and I step out to play
along this lane an autumn day

Dying leaves will lose their hold
as thinning vines like arms unfold
and there a windswept blanket lay
when rain returns and leaves decay

Please stay colors bright and bold
a fiery blaze before the cold
Sunlight fills the sky today
Vineyard leaves a grand display ⚘

Zucchini Bread

Silver sky warns rain
Basket in hand
I rush to the garden
Red tomatoes
past their prime
glow amber

Thirsty leaves
cling to sleeves
Sticky fingers sort
twist, tug
until I've collected
enough

Cucumbers long gone
allow dandelions
to dwell
in dried out pools
The garden is done
I say aloud

Always more zucchini
One long as my arm
hides among stems
strong as celery ribs
shreds to exactly
three cups ❧

Meatloaf

They sit cross-legged on the floor
photo album spread between them
laughter like wind chimes
The story of our lives before
she arrives

I know my meatloaf recipe
pungent onions, garlic,
bread crumbs, ketchup, and egg
For the girl something new
brown sugar and sage ♣

Milk Clouds Cauliflower

Snow
swans
frost
sea foam

Milk clouds
cauliflower

Rice
salt
sugar
bones

Soap bars
polar bears

Ghosts
doves
pearls
gloves

Tissue
wedding dress

White ♣

Seascape

Wavelets clip the tide
Small black-winged birds
draw horizontal lines

Gray is not gray
Gray is silver brown lavender
Shadows breathe deep and shallow

The seagull lifts
Whoosh   ♣

A Grape Mystery

Grapes at the grocery
are sour or sweet
Which colorful bunch
should I pick to eat

Red, purple, green
How will I know
My eyes cannot taste
Taste does not show

I should not steal
but money is tight
I can't go home
without picking what's right

The bins are all full
No one would know
If one grape goes missing
how can it show

Soon as I reach out
my fingers to pluck
a produce clerk waves
I'm out of luck

I know her quite well
shop this store weekly
Now I am sure

I can't be sneaky

Shyly, I ask
which grapes are sweet
Try one she says
They're ready to eat ♣

Blue Sea

pulls gold
sand round
pink toes

Beach sinks
leaves feet
for next wave

Run

Betty's Black Bible

My hands smooth the coarse black cloth
open the book back to front
Hebrew letters march right to left like obedient soldiers
An index card yellowed by age slips out
 Dear ones died
 Mollie (Mulshi) Goldstein died June 9, 1962 sister
  74 yrs.
 Freddy (Fragel) Aaron died Mar. 26, 1981 sister
  69 yrs.
 Nathan (Nusson) Sperling died Dec. 27, 1930
  brother
Yiddish names are hard to say even to myself
 Morris...
 Abe...
 Howard...
 Gladys...
After sixteen names the empty space is daunting
Grandma was Bubbe but I never called her that
Betty (Sperling) Friedman, October 28, 1996

It's time I took over

A Certain Blue

Forget-me-not the blue of his eyes
by the fluttering of a blue jay's wing
or Caribbean pools remembering

His gaze of star-flecked turquoise stone
a pendant near my heart
offers me his loyalty whenever we're apart

Bound to me by destiny
however long eternity
this blue I know with certainty ♣

Dusting Mother after She's Gone

Smiling through glass
Trapped in frame
Mother

Cloth
touching
dust ♣

Under the Bed

Extra shoes in case of earthquake
Baseball bat in case of attack
Gift wrap storage container

Native American rug
given to me by my dad
given to him by a friend
*Please keep this for me
until I come back*
Dad promised
took the man's treasures
They became ours
A rug, bull whip,
and a sleek oak desk
I loved how the desk
added class
to our living-room

As a twelve-year-old
no one explained to me
where the man went
Draft dodger
or to war in Vietnam
Perhaps he escaped
a bad relationship
or found a new one

He never returned
Years later after Dad died
the rug shipped to me

I just found a second baseball bat
What will I do with two bats
Backup for the first bat
My husband says
Oh, and one sock
There is always a sock
under the bed
where socks go
if they are hiding
from the sock-eating
monster who lives
in the laundry room

I pull the rug out
examine frayed corners
small holes in wool
research geometric patterns
find symbols which bring
good fortune
Let's have it appraised
my husband says
and have it restored
For now the man's
unfinished story remains
under the bed ✤

Blessed

Freckles and age spots
They all look the same
Darn brownish dots
The sun is to blame

Some opt for makeup
Some just complain
Some try to scrub
The permanent stain

When seen on a child
freckles are sweet
Often I smile
whenever we meet

All over the face
and the back of a hand
Woven like lace
Sprinkled like sand

Like pennies to find
in all sorts of places
A coppery shine
instead of plain spaces

No use to protest
when age spots appear
Instead to be blessed
with proof we're still here ♣

When we go to Lunch

We shall all wear hats
and long floral skirts in the garden
We'll sip lavender tea and sparkling wine
and agree to surrender our burdens

When we go to lunch we shall trust that our hats
hold most of our secrets within
We'll eat all our words from silver spoons
and tighten silk bows at our chins

All of our hats shall have a wide brim
to protect the aging of skin
All of our hats shall shadow raised brows
from the gossip we revel in

When we go to lunch we shall try other hats
stylish or garish or sweet
When we go to lunch we shall dare all our hats
to flee when we sit down to eat ♣

Light the Way

Sunlight, morning light,
daylight, moonlight,
starlight

Candlelight, nightlight,
lamplight, low light,
flashlight

Lightweight, light-footed,
light-headed, lighthearted,
light-colored

Porch light, street light,
headlight, taillight,
stoplight

Brake light, turn light,
red light, green light,
yellow light

Lighthouse, light show
light bulb, light up,
lights out ♣

Walking the Labyrinth

(In memory of Anne)

One foot in front of the other
experiencing and sharing its beauty
Slowing down
Being in touch with Mother Earth
In great company and energy

The earth beneath my feet
stirs my inner journey

Prayer is such a simple thing
a gift to send to Anne
She is here
says the wind

As I train my mind to listen
a little bird cocks its head
At last I notice

Looking up from the path to spy
rocky curves ahead of me
throws me into fear of failing
until I see the path knows

Memorial stones inspire
Live in the now
It is home

Moving through circles
my destination being center
this uneven trail like life
I go within
Breathe
I am present

The Labyrinth clears
Answers are profound
meaningful and beautiful
Notice the shadows intertwined
among friends and the setting sun ♣

*by Barbara Toboni with contributing members of Napa
Meditation Circle: Jacqueline Eigen, Donna DeWeerd, Marlene
Gerosa, Jackie Fisher, Jean Cullinane, Sharyn Fuller, Vivienne
Brandi, and Jessie McDermott*

Lady: Dog by the Creek

(1996-2010)

This is where the black lab spent
her last days before she
refused food, company
yet something was here for her

Ears perked to twittering birds
cadence of water rippling
she licked one arthritic paw
as if to heal old age

Calmed in a nest
of wet grass and oak leaves
Inside the peace of this place
Lady recalled beloved memories
lively walks, squirrel hunts
pats and treats
befriending the postman

Lady thrilled in long drives north
lapping water in tree-lined lakes
frosted paws padding snow

This creek sent for her
as if her young boy master
still splashed about

chased her over mossy rocks
graveled bank and root hollow

Lady knew this path
It called her home ❖

Lament

We were going to do this together
Write every day, play, create
Every morning I am present
pages pristine
ready to serve
Where are you
afraid of false starts, failure
Remember when Lady dog died
that poem you wrote
I saved the tear-stained page
Remember lonely nights
writing in circles till dawn
random thoughts
I still feel the pen spinning
Without you I have nothing to say
I'm only space for mind maps and detours ♣

Words for Sale

If you don't read my emails
then what should I do with all these words
Store them in boxes
Move them from room to room
until they reach the garage

Bring them out in the spring
to the front yard
WORDS FOR SALE
Use them to write signs
or create lists

I could give them to a thrift shop
No. I couldn't bear to hear them
spilling out
of a secondhand mouth

I could throw them out into the street
No. They might get stuck
on someone's shoe
like chewing gum

One thing for sure
I can't use them for emails anymore
The only solution is to bury them
At least they will be good
for filling in black holes ♣

Do You Know

First time I realized
I had a problem with *ya know*
I was in a college speech class

We were assigned
an oral speech, *ya know*
using a visual aid and index cards, *ya know*

I delivered my speech
which was based on a lecture
from my sociology class, *ya know*

About the style of neighborhoods
contributing to the behavior of neighbors, *ya know*
Fascinating stuff, *ya know*

A friend drew my visual aid
because I'm not an artist, *ya know*
I never told anyone that, *ya know*

Or about my awful grade, a "D"
after all that work, *ya know*
My teacher said I overused *ya know*

Now you know my secret
and you know my grade
So, *ya know,* what do you think? ♣

Curse You Computer

And your microchips too
May they turn into nachos
dripping with goo

Curse you computer
with your cursor a-blinking
May your data dissolve
as the hard drive stops thinking

Curse you computer
and your email box too
May you develop a virus
most voracious to you

Curse you computer
and your functioning keys
I shall soak them in soda
and clog them with grease

Curse you computer
and your foul clicking mouse
May he move from the mouse pad
right into your house

Curse you computer
You inhuman freak
You stole my husband
and gave me a geek ♣

Rock's Dilemma

Once I was stuck
Rock wedged
in a hard place

You are
paralyzed
she said

I am Rock
So what

She pushed Rock
uphill
Rock and roll
she whispered
letting go

HELP

ROCK!
ROLL
she yelled

Rock flew
split, chipped
couldn't stop
pebbling ♣

Stomp

Rock flattened
to sand

Bits slipped inside her shoe
freeing Rock to go anywhere ✤

Traffic Jamming

We call them the Wheeler family
Follow their trailer full of wheeled belongings
toy trucks, bikes, coolers, and tubs
back into town

Usually we whiz right by here
Now we can see everything
including the wings on a lady bug
A joke, but it's true

Hot pink poppies
in the golden brush
Signs: Step in Taste our Zin
DINER, Biscuits and Gravy
CLOSED

A rusty garden of metal sculptures
A real garden
Trucks and tractors stand
in their oxidized frames
of another generation

At the Vineyard Hotel
swimming pool
nobody swims
and the little magnolia tree
blooms big and white
at its center

Up ahead
white Suburban
leaves big gap in line
The nerve
of some people

Cherry stands make us hunger for dinner
The Boon Fly Café has the best sign
OPEN ♣

Face the World

Age sprightly
Rejuvenate
Flower to bud
again
I'm only one bottle
of wrinkle repair
away

Nightly creams
daily potions
tiny jars
solutions
keep my cells
alive
longer

Fearing
free radicals
in "cosmeceuticals"
Botox needles
surgical knives
I drape all
mirrors
Hide under
my bed

Derm doctors
what are you doing?
Creating elasticity
for my face?
Sorry
This is not
a rubber ball ♣

Off the Rack

It flows from a hanger
A scarf is all it is with a slip underneath
I can dress this up with jewelry
No. Dress this down with slippers
It's a nightgown gone looking for a rendezvous
Yet I'm fond of the beachy pattern
brown swirl of waves
ruffles on a diagonal across the bodice

I dance Scarf to the changing room
along with a bouquet of possibilities
A sleeveless empire dress
white piping on navy
hibiscus and poinsettia blooms
but not at all Hawaiian
and a stretchy red tee
scrunched at the neckline

Red tee fits
just as I suspected
The mirror calls attention
to my bustline
stresses the importance
of having one
Empire is more like it
or like it once was

I slip Scarf over my head
and the brown flounce speaks
"Let's dance"
I say, "Not now"
"Let's flirt"
I say "How inappropriate"
Finally the whole dress shifts to one side
blurts out, "Let's be spontaneous"
I hiss back, "That's enough"
I don't need some gutsy garment
to tell me what to wear ♣

What Lily Sees from Her Flower Pot

When the weather is mild Mrs. sits in the porch swing
or eats lunch at the round glass table
If she forgets to bring something to read she
    admires me
with a smile once reserved for her boys
though they broke the garden window
and made up a silly lie to tell their parents
A bird dove into it

Mr. saves rain water in a metal can for me that I share
with my bloomies, Azalea and Zinnia
Whenever he's around I try to look my best
lean into the sun a little, try to look appreciative
though I prefer shade
On warm afternoons he naps nearby
I feel him breathing

Mrs. rarely comes out now, not even with her
    yellow broom,
the bristles bent, the handle scarred from sword fights
though the boys should have done chores
We miss her humming over
our show, pink lace fluttering with grace
tangerine tutus in beat with the breeze
We miss Sunday barbecues

Some days on her way to the mailbox, Mrs. stops at
    the roses
but doesn't sniff

She sorts mail at the glass table and gazes out at the yard
as if looking for mischief
an old habit she's not willing to pass
though the boys left that busted backboard for hoops
with their explanation long forgotten ✤

Dear Walmart Girl

When you approached our car in the parking lot
"Excuse me, can you spare some change?"
I thought, *At Walmart?*
We are shopping at a discount store
We are cheaper folks than most

I answered quickly before my husband, David, a prince,
could oblige you, a damsel in distress
"No, we don't have any spare change."
A lie. I was just inside the store and the clerk
had given me ninety-six cents worth of coins, and I
    thought
What will I do with all of this
I should have dumped my change purse into your hands
My load would have been lighter, yours too, or heavier
Would I be supporting a drug habit

You see, my intentions were good
I wanted to protect David, the kind of man people
take advantage of, a soft touch, an easy target
a man that picks up the phone and listens to
    telemarketers
always giving them a chance
Dogs, cats, and children know this
I know too

When we take walks, David picks up lost objects—
something I would never do—places them where the
   owners
might find them, the top of a gate, or the lid of a trash
   can
What if you are not a drug addict
What if, because we didn't
help you, you went home to some awful situation
What if your parents abandoned you
What if your husband mistreated you

Now, you haunt me
I imagine you sitting alone on that bench outside the
   store
sunburned face turned away from our car as we leave
   Walmart
David shouting, "HEY, GIRL! WALMART GIRL!"
Coins flying out his window ✢

Pinching Pennies is a Good Thing

Find a penny pick it up
All the day you'll have good luck
Flip mats, mattresses
couch cushions
On laundry day
search everyone's pockets
Scoop me out of rain puddles

Find a penny put it in your
shoe. You'll have luck
the whole day through
A better plan
plunk me in a can
jar or piggy bank
Let your feet thank me

A penny saved is a penny earned
Collect, tally, fill a roll
Suit me in a paper sleeve
Leave me at the bank
You can nurture our future

Every time it rains
It rains...
Pennies from Heaven
In showers
I blush copper

A penny for your thoughts
Two cents worth
of opinion
What a deal

Lucky penny
Drop me in the fountain, wish me well
because when you let me go
you see sunlight and moonlight
water rippling, glistening stars
There are no bad pennies
You are worth every cent

Points of Light

Dusk at the golf course
Chairs prop, blankets billow, sodas pop
Footballs, Frisbees, and flags fly
A pretty woman winds her hair
in a red bandanna
Children don circles of dazzling light

Boom!
Reds, whites, and blues
arc the darkened sky
Teens race for a better view
as fiery ribbons bloom
gold stars liquefy

Beyond the rolling lawns
awe-struck crowd
in the Veteran's Hospital
I'm told PTSD patients
can't shake the madness
of our merriment ♣

Flying

Once I dreamed of flying
mastered the art
Launched from a hilltop
arms outstretched
Trusted the sky
to keep me aloft

Let's go, I whispered
Featherless
I swooped, swayed
looped and played
with falling
The breeze loved me

Unafraid
I looked down
Folks pointed
waved, hollered
I heard
See there?
Isn't it easy? ✤

Acknowledgements

My sincere thanks to my writing group, Patsy Ann Taylor, Amber Lea Starfire, Marilyn Campbell, and Sarita Lopez for their patience and skill in critiquing my work. Also, a special thank you to Amber Lea Starfire for her professional help in book formatting and design.

For my family and friends, thank you for your encouragement and support, especially my husband, David, for his willingness to stop whatever he is doing in order to listen to me read my poetry.

About the Author

Barbara Toboni is the author of two previous collections of poetry, *Undertow* and *Water Over Time.* Her award-winning poems have appeared in print and online. Her children's book, *The Bunny Poets,* will be released in 2018 by MacClaren-Chocrane Publishing. The author lives in Napa, California with her husband.

http://barbaratoboni.com/

❧

57805499R00046

Made in the USA
San Bernardino, CA
23 November 2017